Preface

Dear Reader,

The book you hold in your hands does not aspire to be a traditional manual, nor a simple tutorial.
Here, you will not find canonical rules about the proportion of letters, nor detailed explanations on the inclination of strokes, or the fundamental aspects that define the various writing styles.
There will be no guides on how to create calligraphic tools, nor advice on which ink to choose, which paper is best, or how to maintain the ideal posture while writing. The market already has excellent learning tools for these needs, and the purpose of my book is distinctly different from being a copy of these manuals or assuming an academic tone.

However, I invite you to approach this fascinating world with methodical study, meticulous attention to details, daily dedication, and tireless curiosity, but above all, with a personal and genuine approach. Artistic freedom is wonderful, but, although vast and seemingly limitless, it needs a well-defined perimeter to avoid slipping into chaos.

Knowing the rules, learning the proportions, the spacings, the inclinations, and the shapes of each letter and each style is just the first step on a much larger ladder.
The real artistic journey begins when you start to make this knowledge your own, when you begin to bend and reshape the rules to create something absolutely unique and personal.

The letters you create today are the mirror of your inner journey, your vision, your essence.
They will evolve with you, gaining more solidity, confidence, and maturity over time.
They will become the visual story of who you are.
These pages are the result of countless hours spent drawing, repeating the same stroke, the same letter, the same word, the same composition.

Today, I am here, not with the intention of teaching, advising, or imparting lessons.
I write this book to share myself, my studies, and my experiences through my letters. And I do so with the hope that these may inspire each one of you to find your own unique voice in the world of letters.

This book is meant to be read, leafed through, consulted over and over, used, and written in.
I hope that in these pages you will find not only inspiration, but also your own path to express yourself through the art of letters, to discover and rediscover the beauty hidden in every stroke, in every curve, in every blank space.

Preface

Biography

I am Stefano Pedruzzi, born in August 1994 in Bergamo, a city in northern Italy. My artistic imprinting began on the walls, where, at just 13 years old, I discovered the expressive power of graffiti.

This initial encounter with art taught me more than I could have imagined: design, proportion, and above all, the strength of manual skill. The streets became my first true school, a place where I could experiment artistically and grow as a person, nurturing traits that would be essential in my future, such as ambition and dedication.

My interest gradually shifted from the vibrancy of colors to the structure of letters.

I began to focus less on effects and more on the pure form of the letter, its anatomy. Calligraphy entered my life as a revelation, seamlessly and gradually leading me into a world where ink and paper replaced spray paint and walls. The tools and mediums changed, but my constant search and study of the letter remained.

My degree in Communication Design from the Politecnico di Milano was not merely an academic journey, but a continuous exploration of the infinite possibilities of the letter, particularly in the commercial realm.

Adding a digital component to my more tangible background, I mastered all the necessary tools to commercialize my artifacts. From here, I began to apply my art on every possible surface: from large walls to elegant handwritten invitations, to digital logos. Each project was a dialogue between myself, the surface, and the letter, always striving to bring a piece of myself into every work.

In 2018, I ventured further, exploring skin as a new medium for my art. Tattooing became a natural extension of my work, allowing me to transform letters into something even more personal and indelible.

I rediscovered the pleasure and challenge of mastering a new tool and medium.

My artistic path is a reflection of my life: a continual commitment to learning and experimentation. Whether it's the stroke of a pen on paper, spray on a wall, the digital touch on a graphics tablet, or the precision of a tattoo needle, each creation is a piece of my journey, a story told through the letter.

Biography

Index

Letters

Aa

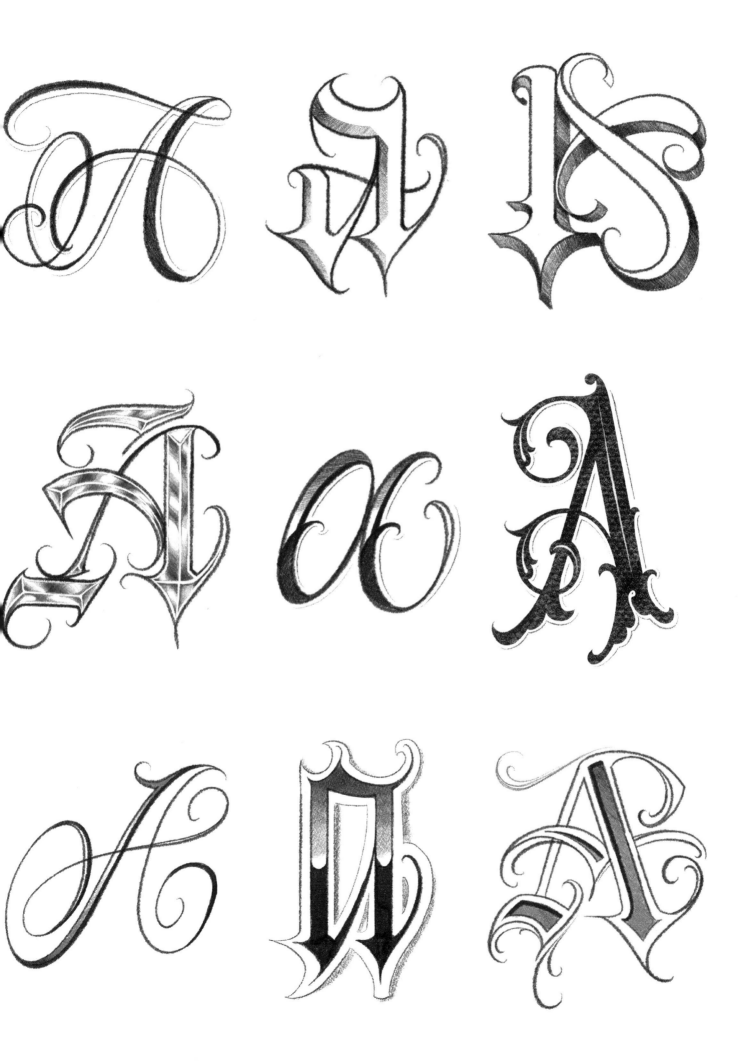

Bb

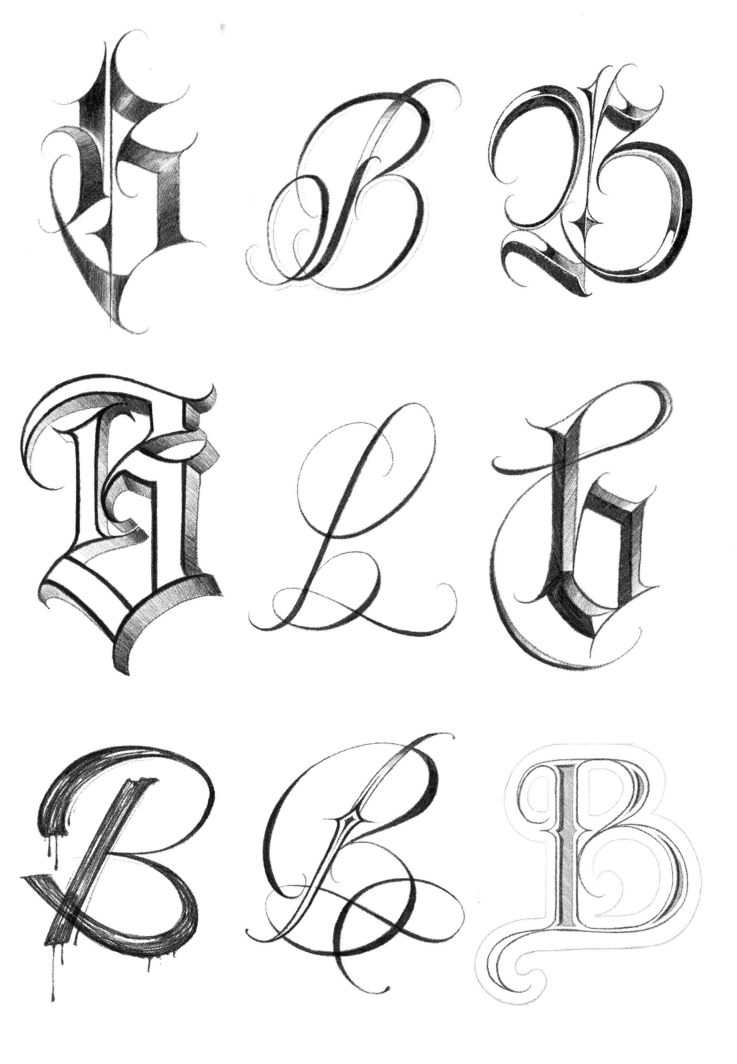

Cc

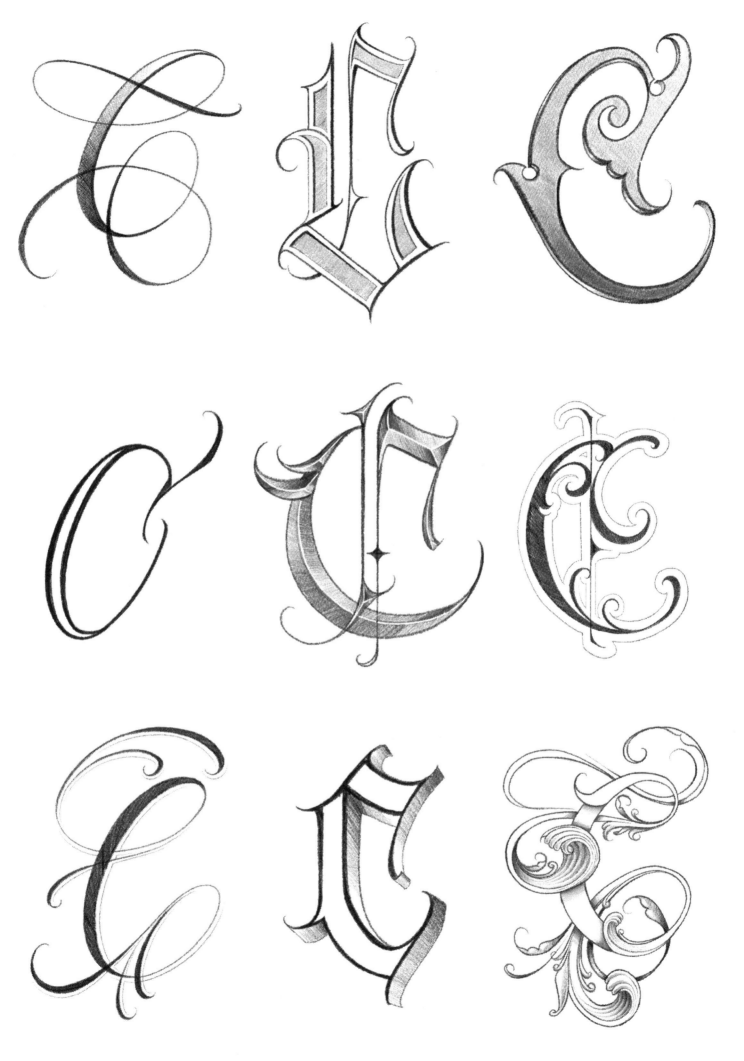

Dd

Ee

Ff

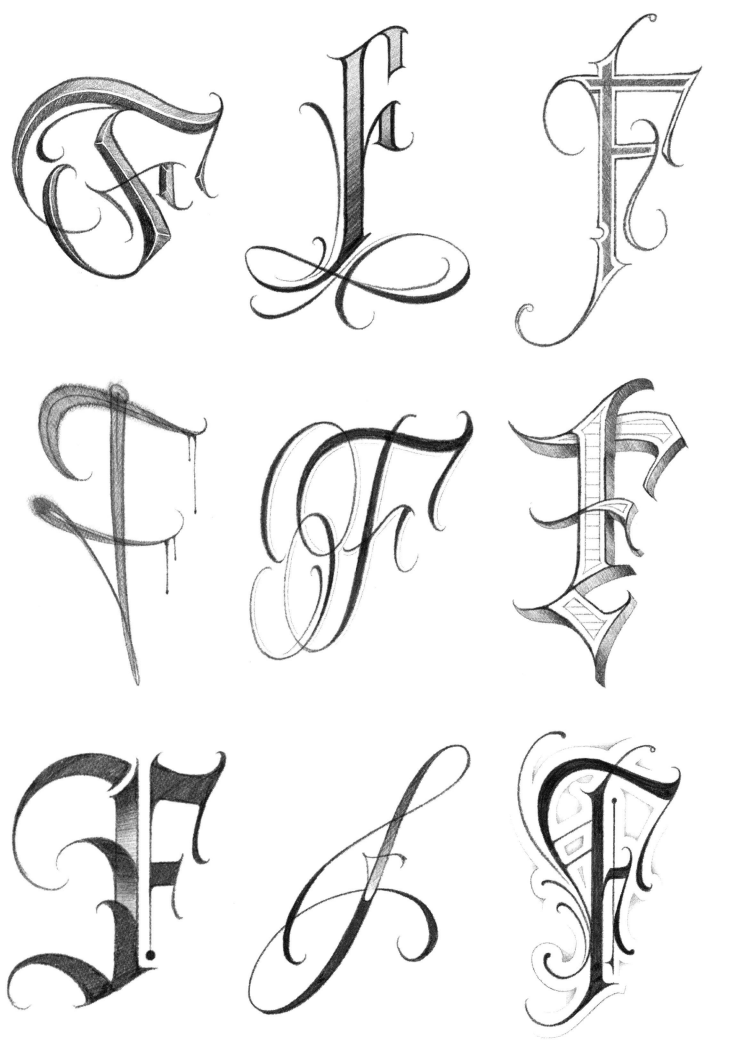

Gg

Hh

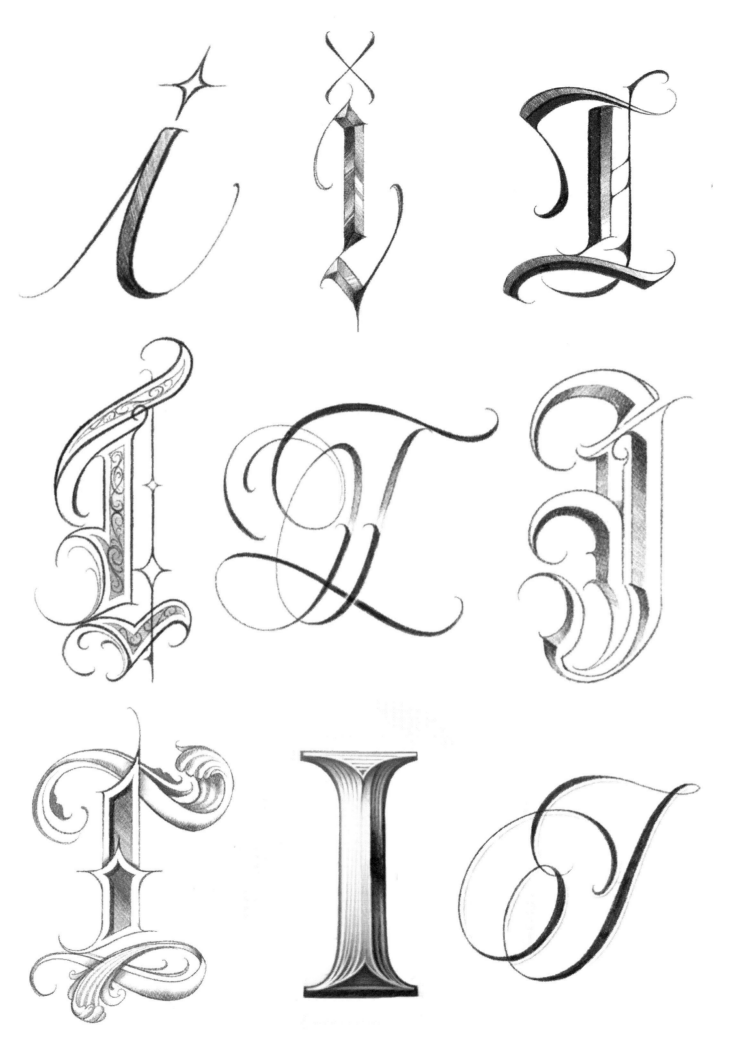

Jj

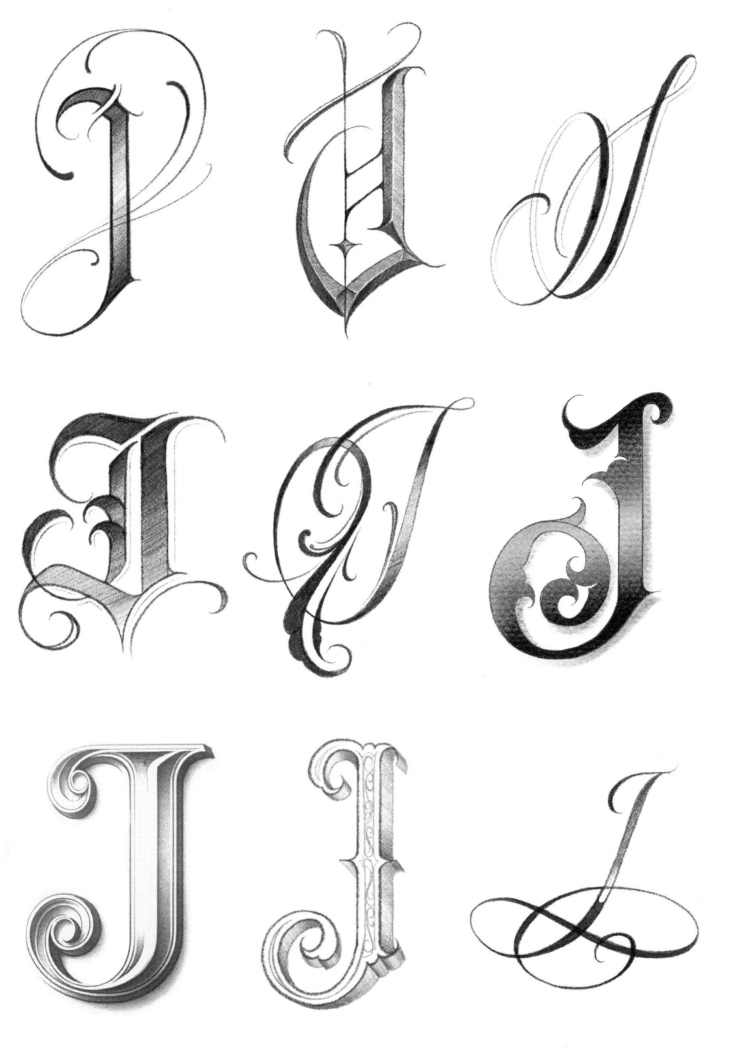

Mm

Nn

Oo

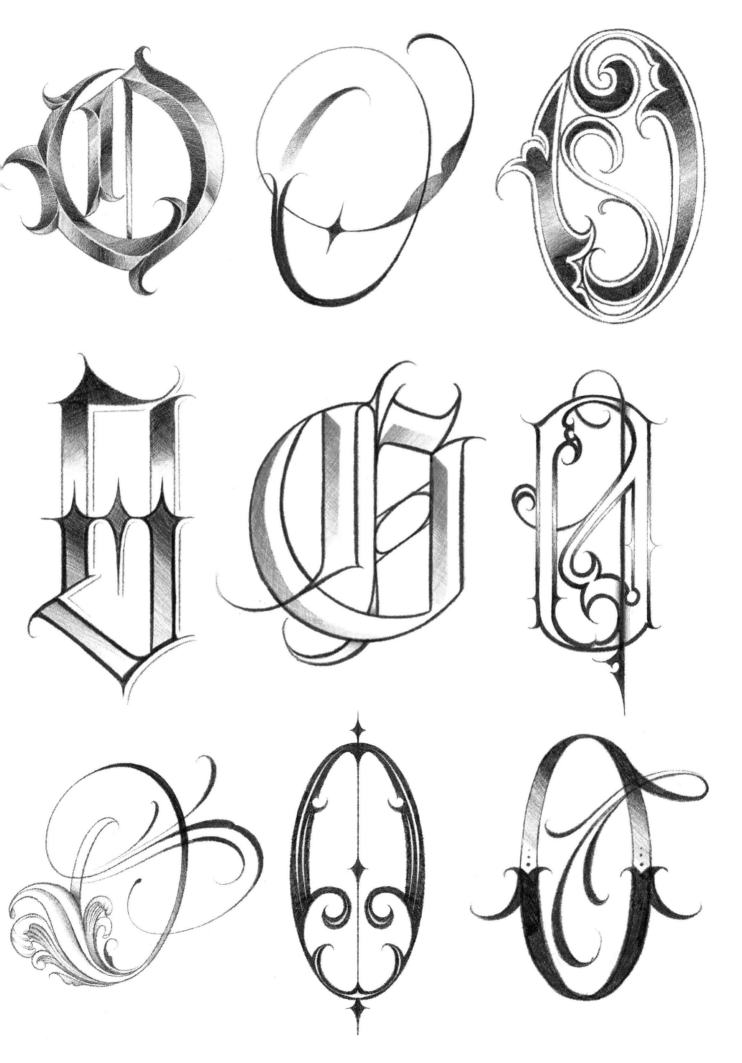

Pp

Qq

Rr

Ss

Tt

Uu

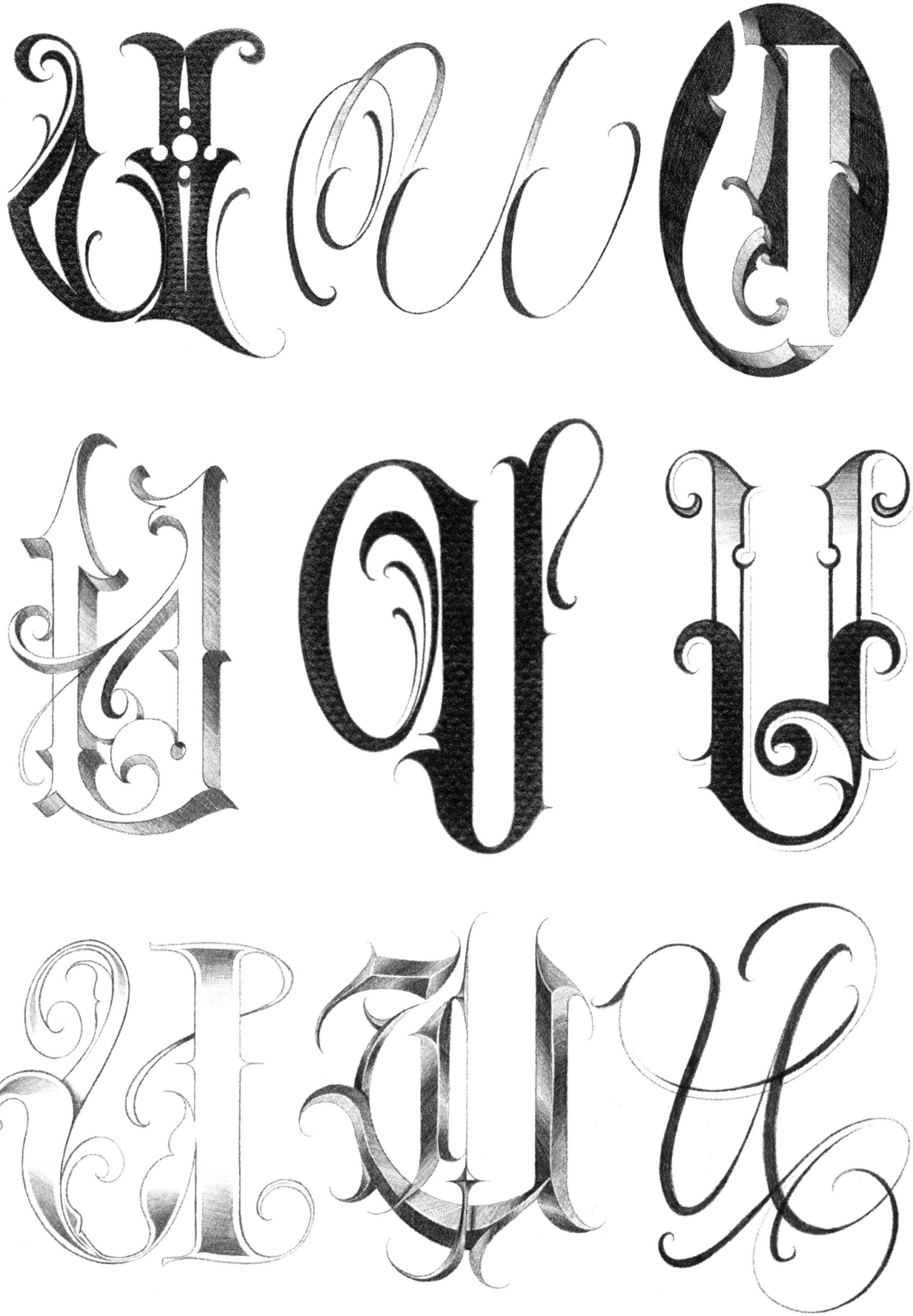

Ww

Zz

Training pages

Aa

Bb

Cc

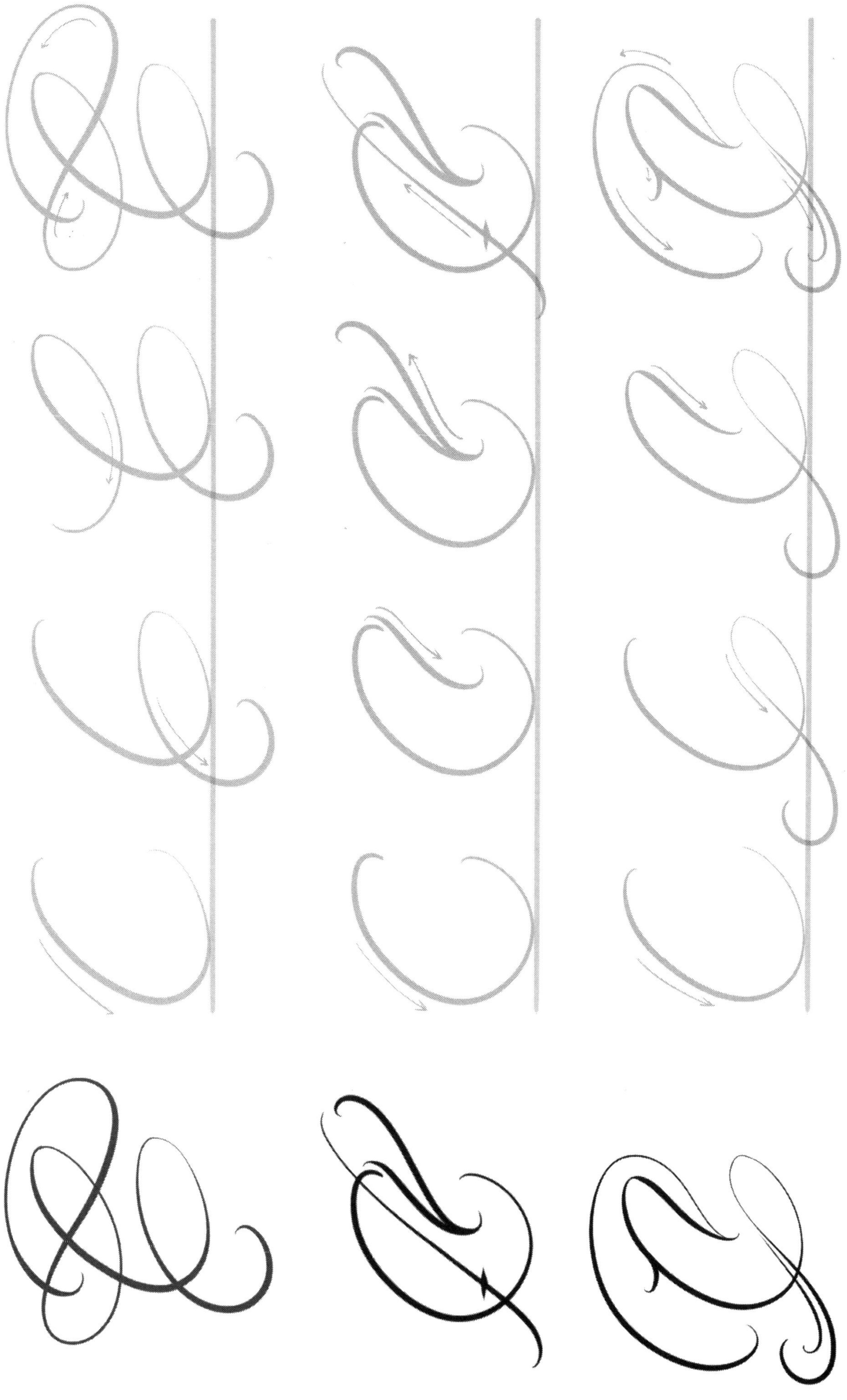

Dd

Ee

Ff

Gg

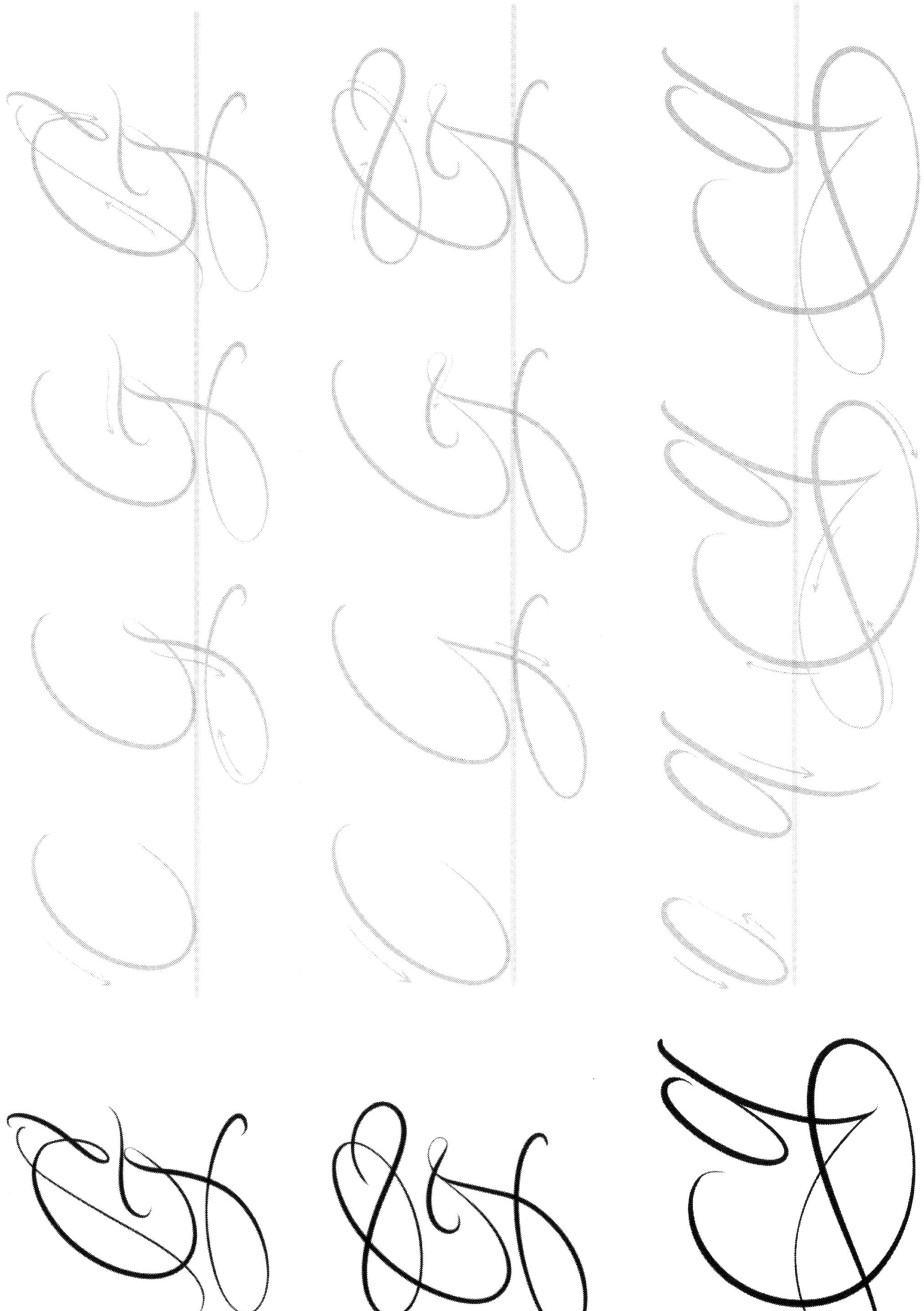

Hh

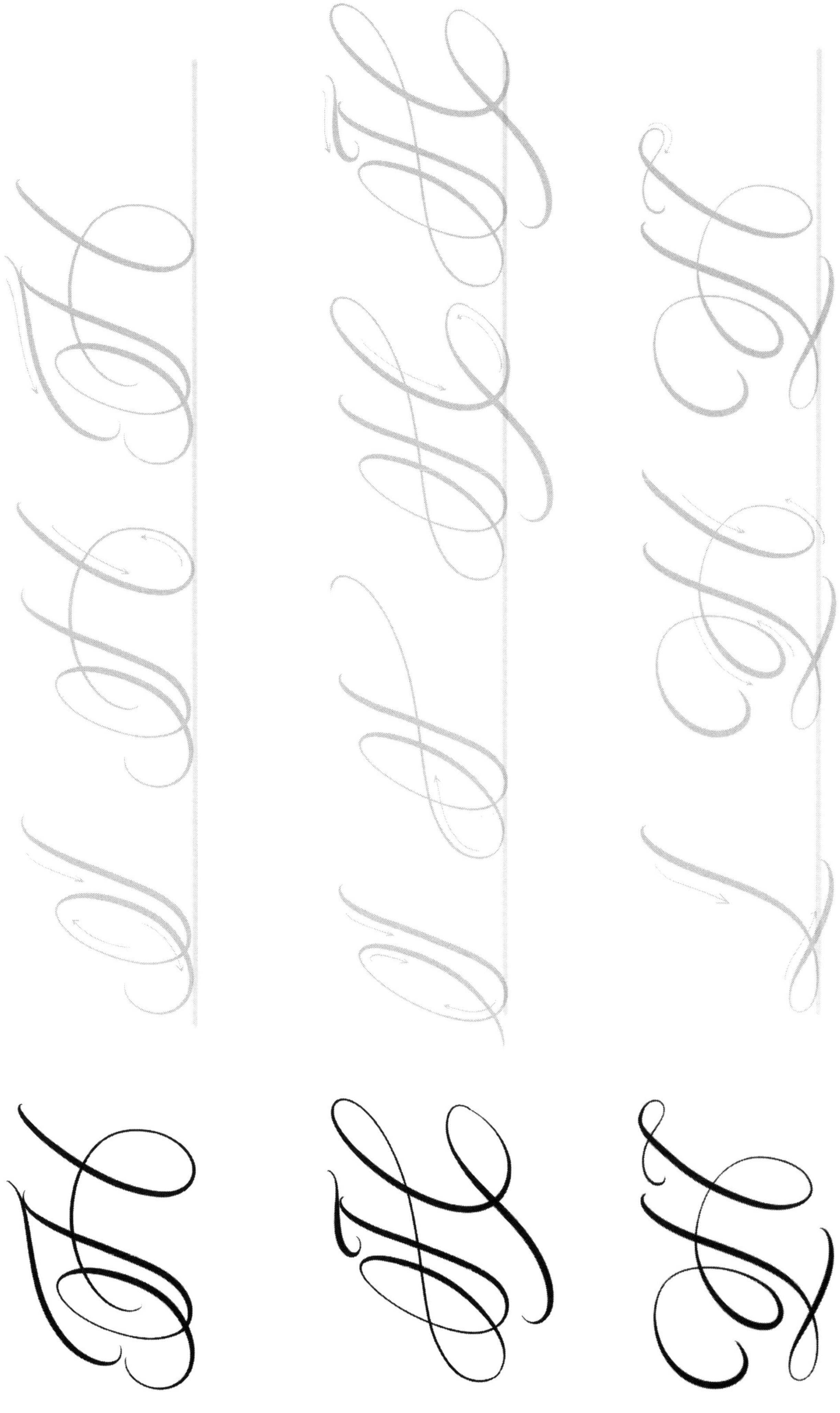

Jj

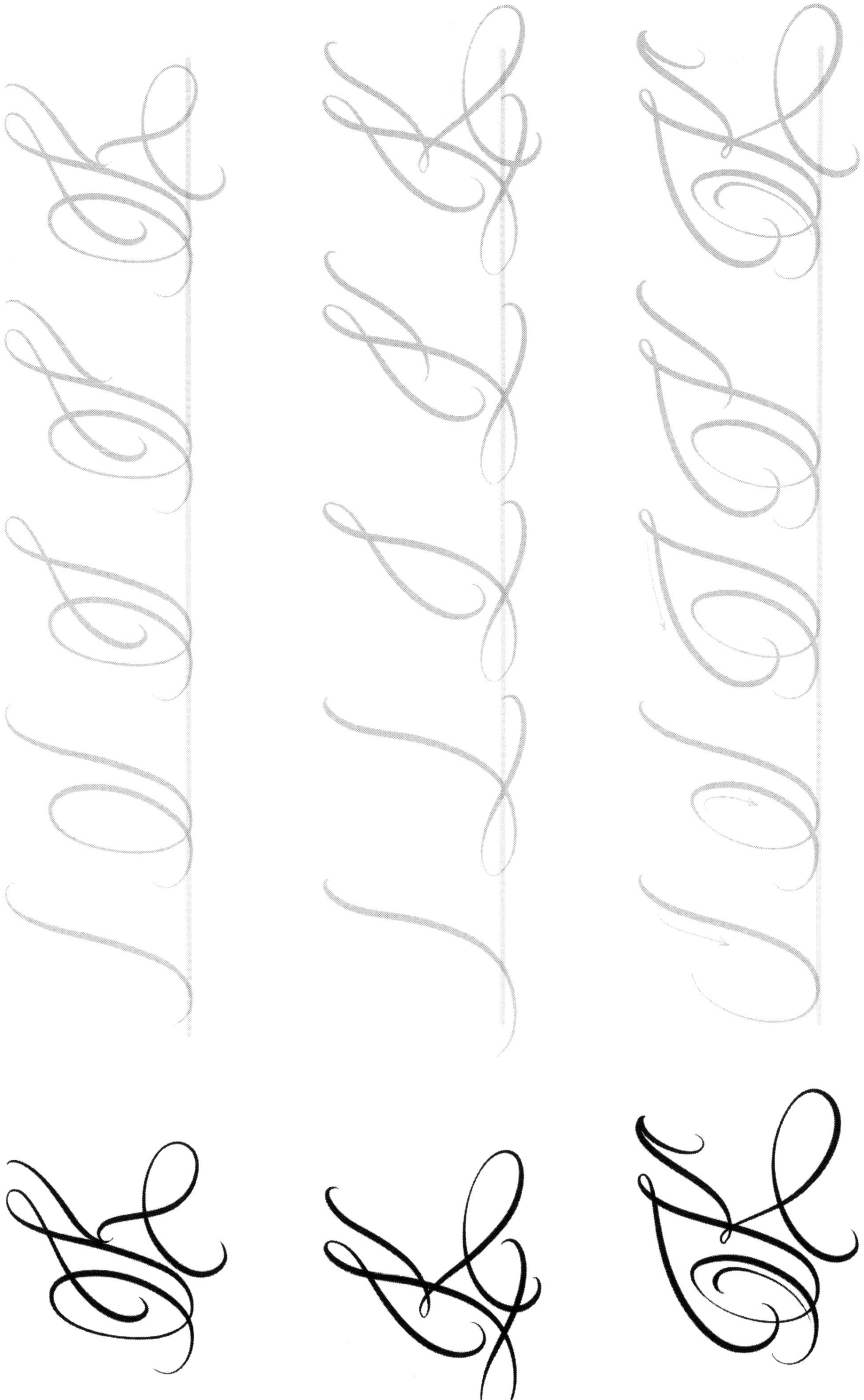

Mm

Nn

Oo

Pp

Qq

Rr

Ss

Tt

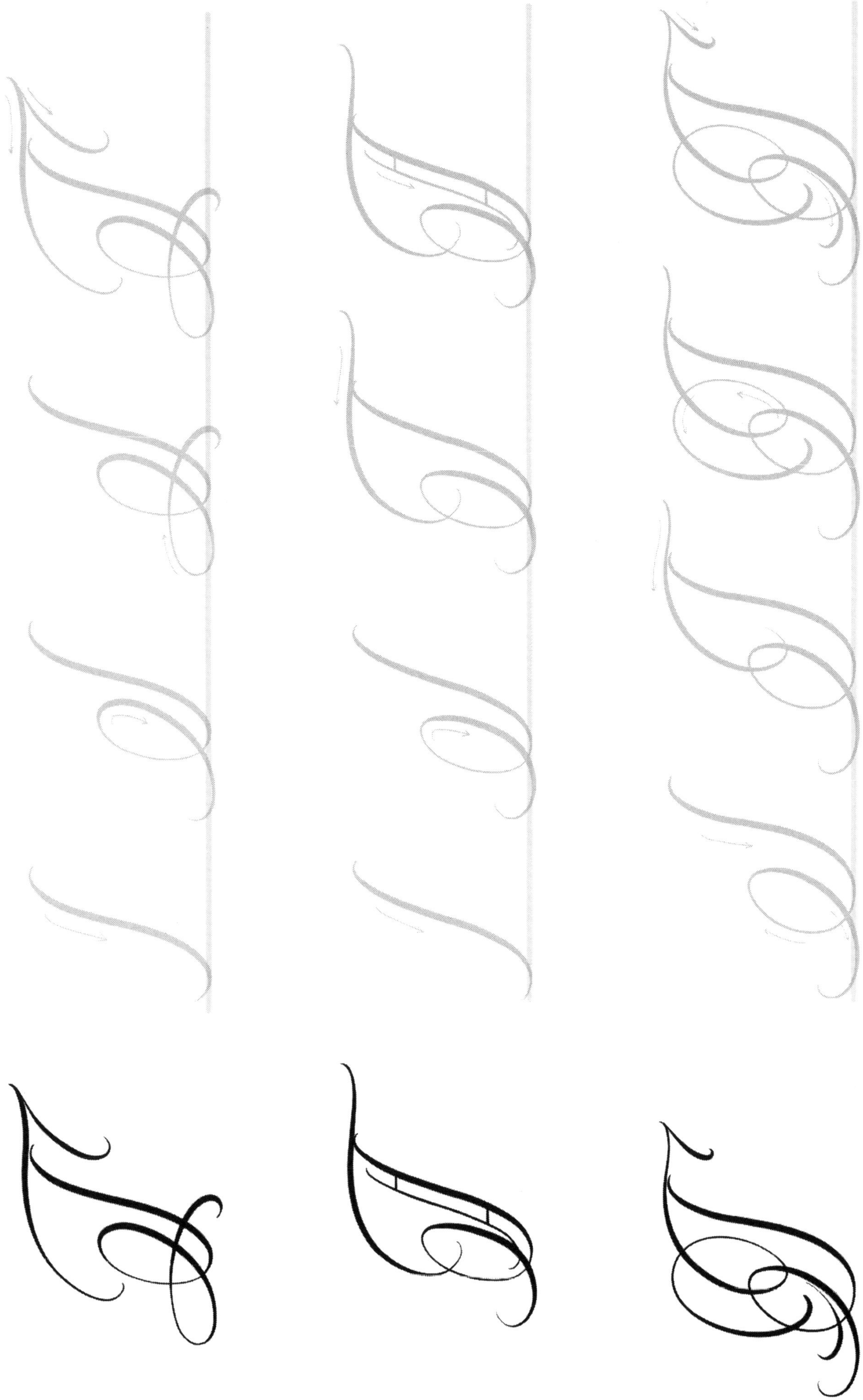

Uu

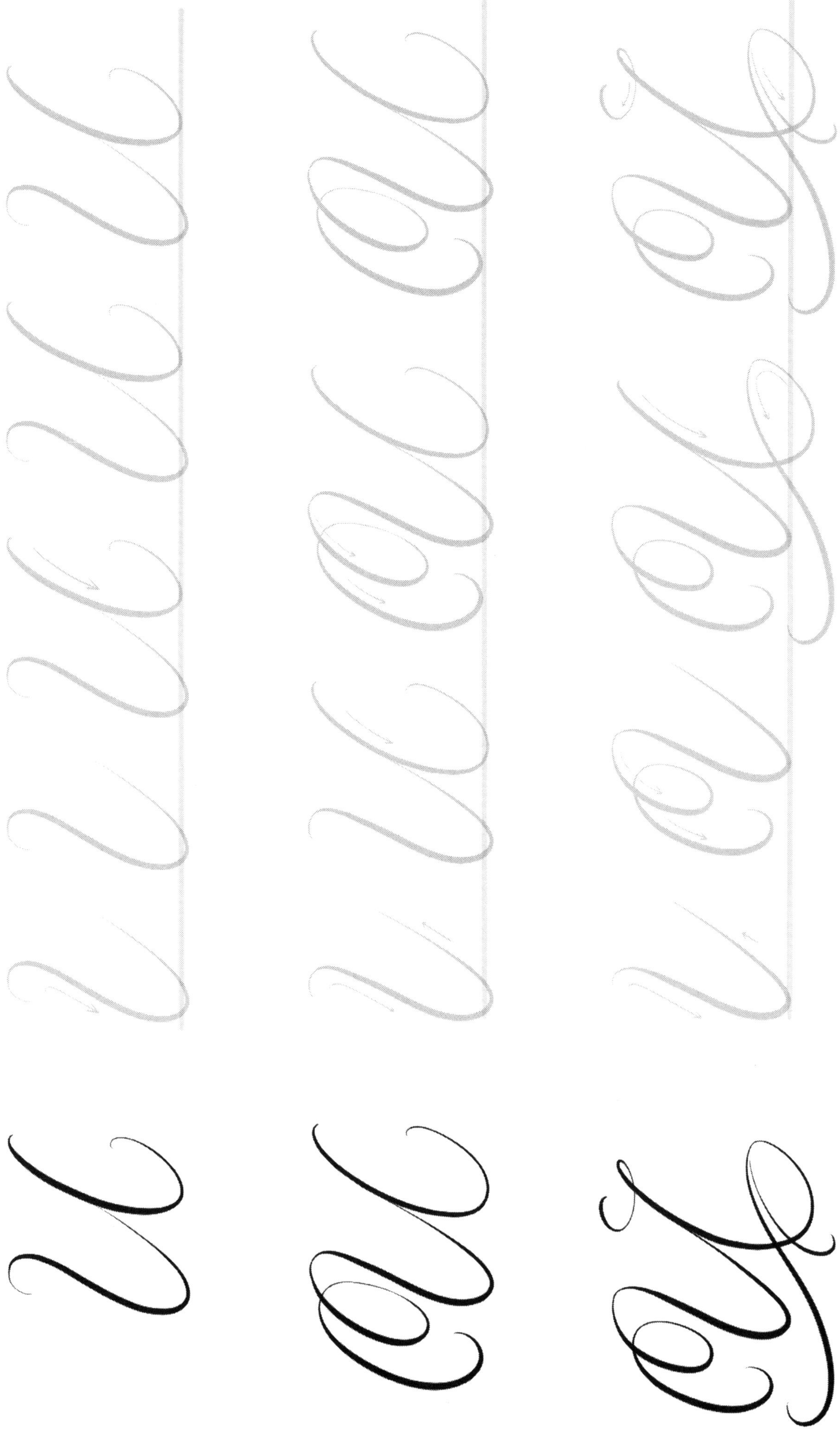

Vv

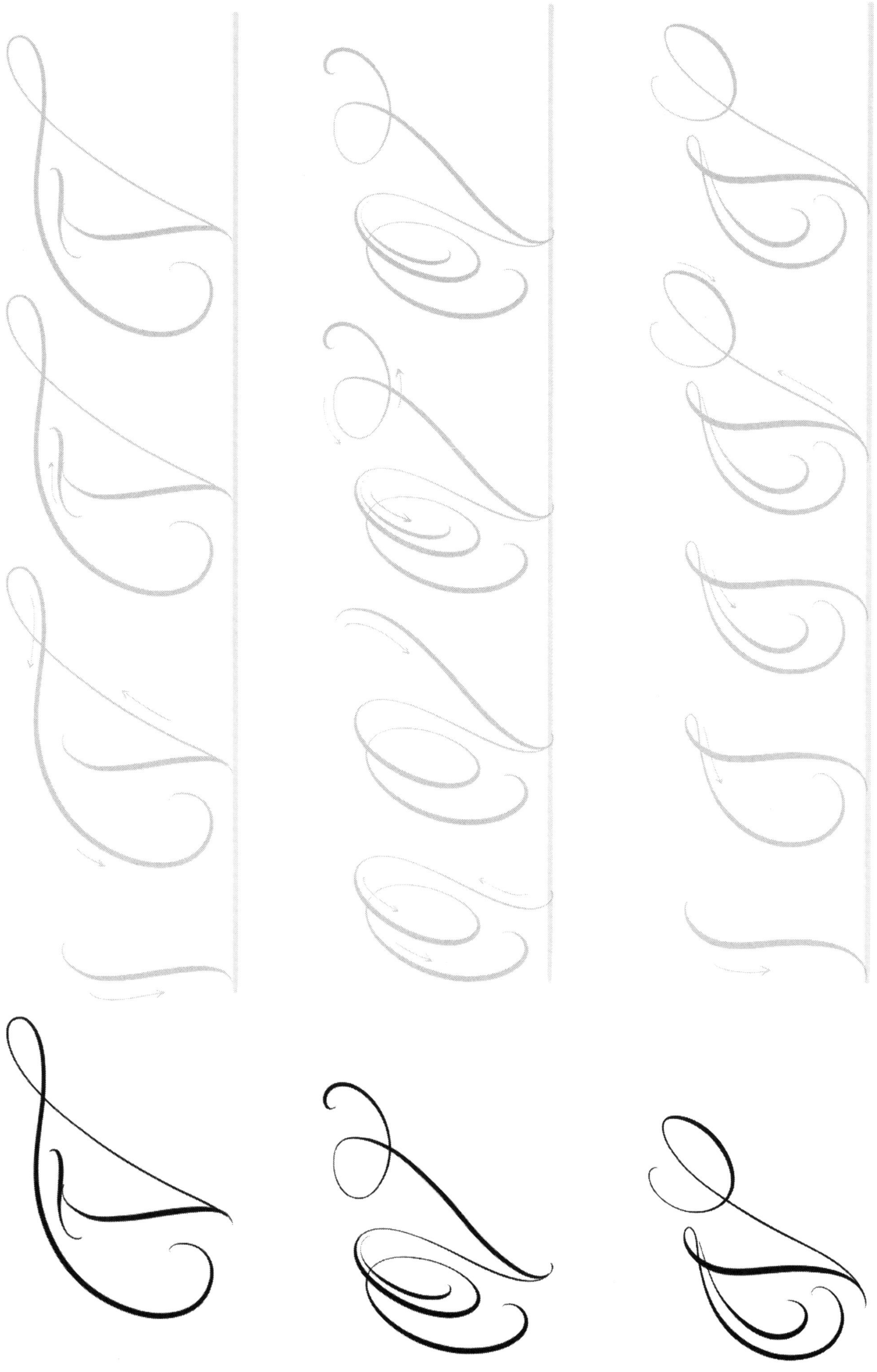

Ww

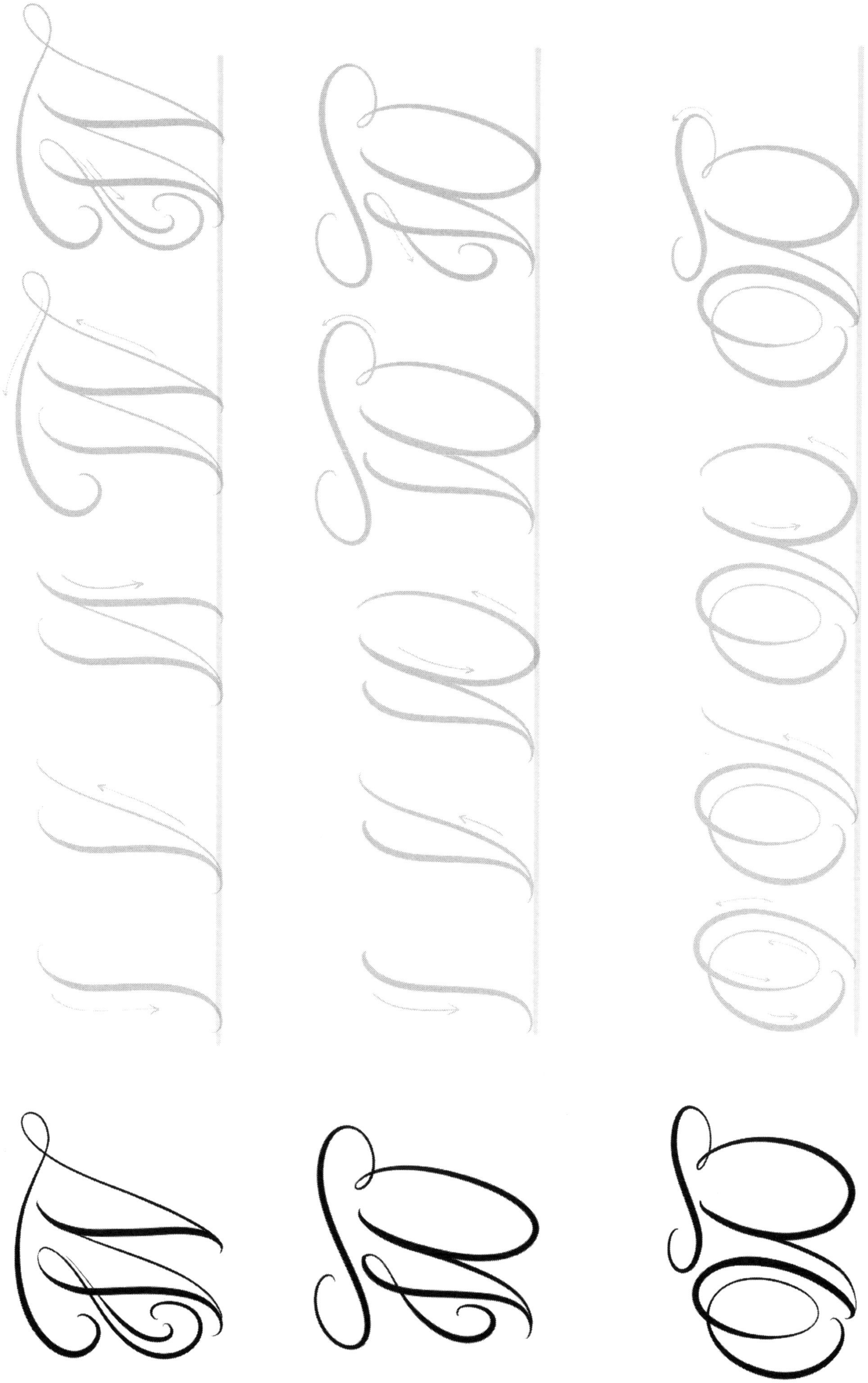

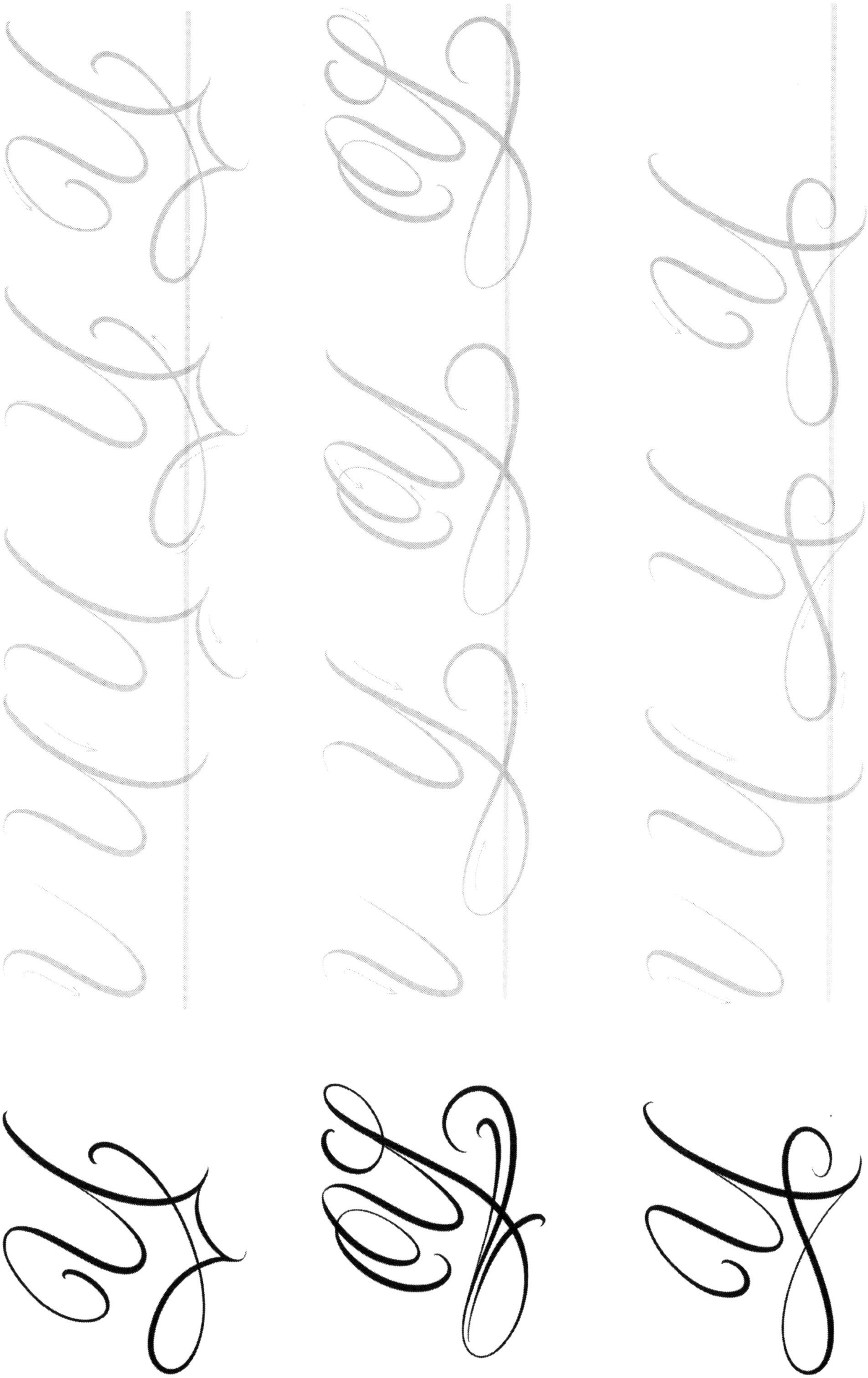

Zz

Flourishes

Introduction to Flourishes

Have you ever been enchanted by the beauty of flourishes? These elaborate ornaments are not just decorations; they are the very soul of many calligraphic styles, particularly in the English Copperplate tradition. Flourishes capture the eye, evoking a sense of elegance and refinement that can transform a simple letter into a work of art.

But what exactly do flourishes represent? They are not merely aesthetic frills, but elements that add depth and character to the text. In this chapter, we will explore not only their history and origin but also their deeper meaning in modern calligraphy.

History and Origins

Have you ever wondered when and where flourishes originated? Their history is as fascinating as their forms. Originally appearing in calligraphy works during the Renaissance, flourishes reached their peak in the English Copperplate calligraphy of the 17th century. This style, known for its elegance and refinement, developed in an era when handwriting was considered a true art form.

Initially, flourishes were used to fill empty spaces in manuscripts and add a personal touch to letters. Over time, they became a means for calligraphers to demonstrate their skill and creativity, transforming into true works of art.

The Nature of Flourishes

Each flourish is an expression of balance and harmony, designed with precise intention. In calligraphy, every line and curve has a purpose, contributing to the overall beauty of the work.

But how are they created? Flourishes require a deep understanding of the shape of the letters and the space around them. It's not just a matter of aesthetics, but also functionality: flourishes must integrate harmoniously with the text, enhancing readability rather than hindering it.

Dynamics and Balance

Every flourish is a play of tensions and relaxations, of lines that extend and retract.

But how is this balance created? It is not a random process. Each curve and counter-curve is calculated to balance the visual weight of the letters. This requires a trained eye and a steady hand, as even the smallest variation can alter the overall harmony of the work. You are called to be both an artist and an architect, constructing compositions that are not only beautiful but structurally sound.

Technique and Variations in Thickness

Have you ever noticed how the stroke of a flourish changes thickness so fluidly and naturally? This is the result of refined technique and a deep understanding of the tool. In calligraphy, each descending and ascending stroke plays a crucial role in defining the shape and style of the flourish.

The key lies in the pressure exerted on the nib. During descending strokes, increased pressure causes the nib tines to open, releasing more ink and creating a thicker line. Conversely, during ascending strokes, lighter pressure allows the tines to close, resulting in a thinner line. This play of pressures requires practice and sensitivity, fundamental elements in mastering the art of flourishes.

Conclusion

Do you now believe that flourishes are mere embellishments? As we have seen, they are much more. They are expressions of history, art, technique, and, above all, passion. Flourishes not only beautify letters; they enrich the meaning and expression of the text.

In the following pages, you will find a small explanatory illustration and some examples that you can replicate following these tips.

Ascending tract
decrease in pressure
thinner tract

Descending tract
increase in pressure
thicker tract

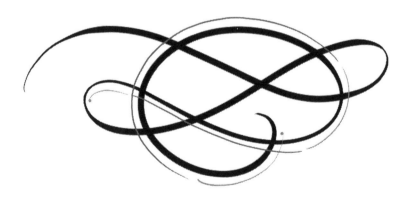

Inspirational words

Altruism

Bravery

Compassion

Determination

Empathy

Forgiveness

Gratitude

Hope

Integrity

Joy

Kindness

Love

Mindfulness

Nobility

Optimism

Philanthropy

Quintessence

Resilience

Serenity

Tenacy

Understanding

Valor

Wisdom

Xenophilia

Yearning

Zeal

Alphabets

A B C D E

F G H A

I K L M N

O P Q R S

T U V W

X Y Z

abcde

fghijkl

mnopqrs

tuvwxy

z

A B C D E

F G H I J

K L M N O

P Q R S T

U V W X Y

Z

abcde

fghij

klmno

pqrst

uvw

xy

z

A B C D

E F G H

I J K L

M N O P

Q R S T

U V W X

Y Z

Sketch Your Vision

Draw your letter, your word, or your phrase, in the style you prefer. Feel free and inspired to create.

And finally, show me your achievements and successes by tagging me on instagram @stephano.lettering.

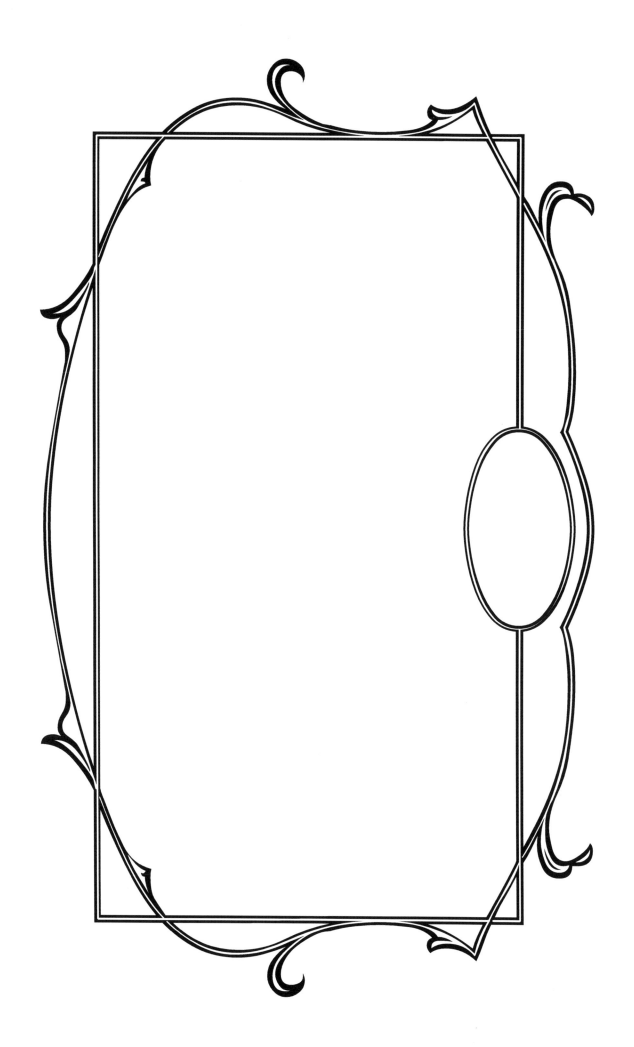

Bonus

Scan QR Code,
Print papers
Start to write

Acknowledgments

To my family, who have always supported me gently, granting me the freedom to make mistakes.

To Ilaria, because we are two out of two.

To Alessandro, the cornerstone of my artistic and life journey.

To Andrea, a true friend and my mentor.

To Laura, because you are here, again.

To Enrico, the younger brother I never had, but now do.

To Charlene, an essential part of this great and beautiful adventure.

To Jiosef, synesthesia and always will be.

To Marco, the simplicity I always need.

To Hamza, for the dedication and consistency I admire in you.

To Luca, we will always be there for each other with the same sincerity.

To Davide, as far as you are, so is my esteem for you.

To Tattoo Ink, my second home.

3193563f-f1be-486f-9445-33c552b4bf90R01